# BLACK BEARS

## JOYCE JEFFRIES

---

**PowerKiDS** press

New York

Published in 2017 by The Rosen Publishing Group, Inc.
29 East 21st Street, New York, NY 10010

First Edition

Editor: Katie Kawa
Book Design: Reann Nye

Photo Credits: Cover, p. 1 Sorin Colac/Shutterstock.com; cover, pp. 1, 3–24 (background) eva_mask/Shutterstock.com; p. 4 Ian Maton/Shutterstock.com; p. 5 (American black bear) Lorraine Logan/Shutterstock.com; p. 5 (Asiatic black bear) kunanon/Shutterstock.com; p. 6 Greg and Jan Ritchie/Shutterstock.com; p. 7 Radu Bercan/Shutterstock.com; p. 8 Chokniti Khongchum/Shutterstock.com; p. 9 C_Gara/Shutterstock.com; p. 10 NaturesMomentsuk/Shutterstock.com; p. 11 critterbiz/Shutterstock.com; p. 12 Anan Kaewkhammul/Shutterstock.com; p. 13 tratong/Shutterstock.com; p. 14 BGSmith/Shutterstock.com; p. 15 Thomas Kitchin & Victoria Hurst/First Light/Getty Images; p. 16 Holly Kuchera/Shutterstock.com; p. 17 Debbie Steinhausser/Shutterstock.com; p. 18 Baranov E/Shutterstock.com; p. 19 Ivan_Sabo/Shutterstock.com; p. 20 apple2499/Shutterstock.com; p. 21 (American black bear) zokru/Shutterstock.com; p. 21 (Asiatic black bear) MaZiKab/Shutterstock.com; p. 22 Wild Art/Shutterstock.com.

Cataloging-in-Publication Data

Names: Jeffries, Joyce.
Title: Black bears / Joyce Jeffries.
Description: New York : PowerKids Press, 2017. | Series: Bears of the world | Includes index.
Identifiers: ISBN 9781499420326 (pbk.) | ISBN 9781499420340 (library bound) | ISBN 9781499420333 (6 pack)
Subjects: LCSH: Black bear–Juvenile literature.
Classification: LCC QL737.C27 J44 2017 | DDC 599.78'5–d23

Manufactured in the United States of America

CPSIA Compliance Information: Batch #BS16PK: For Further Information contact Rosen Publishing, New York, New York at 1-800-237-9932

# CONTENTS

Did you know that not all black bears are black? Some are gray, some are brown, and a small number of them are white! The American black bear is the most common bear found in North America, and American black bears can be all these colors and more.

Another kind of black bear lives in Asia. It's called the Asiatic black bear. This bear is much less common than the American black bear. Your best chance to see one is in a zoo.

cinnamon bear

## — Bear Basics —

A cinnamon bear is a kind of American black bear with brown fur.

These bears might look different, but they're all black bears!

American black bear

Asiatic black bear

# WHERE IN THE WORLD?

The American black bear is a North American bear. American black bears live as far north as Alaska and Canada. They live as far south as Mexico. They also live throughout the **continental** United States—especially in the Northeast and the West.

Asiatic black bears live in small groups throughout parts of Asia. They're found in Southeast Asia, North Korea, South Korea, and Japan. Other groups of Asiatic black bears live in southern and northeastern China. These bears also live in parts of Asia's Himalayan mountain **range**.

North
America

Asia

American black bear

Asiatic black bear

This map shows where American black
bears and Asiatic black bears live.
American black bears live over a much
larger area than Asiatic black bears.

# FANS OF THE FOREST

All black bears are fans of the forest. They like to live in thickly wooded areas with many trees, and they're great tree climbers! These bears can also make their homes in mountain ranges. Some Asiatic black bears live higher in the mountains in summer and move to a lower **elevation** in winter.

American black bears have also been found in **swampy** parts of the southeastern United States. They're sometimes seen around campsites in North America, and they live on the **protected** lands of many U.S. national parks.

black bear claws

Black bears use their sharp claws to climb trees.

# THE AMERICAN BLACK BEAR

American black bears can be different colors **depending** on where they live. While most of these bears have black fur, some bears that live in western North America have brown fur. Certain black bears living in Alaska have fur that looks blue or gray. Black bears with white fur are found in a part of Canada called British Columbia.

Adult American black bears are around 5 to 6 feet (1.5 to 1.8 m) long. Males can weigh up to 600 pounds (272 kg). Females are much smaller than males.

## —Bear Basics—

American black bears with white fur are called Kermode bears. Some Native Americans also call them spirit bears.

American black bears with black fur often have a muzzle that's a lighter color than the rest of their fur. A bear's muzzle is the part of its face that sticks out and includes the mouth and nose.

11

# THE ASIATIC BLACK BEAR

Asiatic black bears have the same dark fur and lighter muzzle as many American black bears, but they don't look exactly the same. Asiatic black bears have a white or sandy-colored "V" on their chest that's easy to spot. They also have longer fur and ears that are farther apart.

Asiatic black bears are generally the same length as American black bears, although they can be a little shorter. They generally weigh less, too. Male Asiatic black bears only weigh up to 440 pounds (200 kg), but that's still very heavy!

## —Bear Basics—
Female Asiatic black bears and female American black bears generally don't weigh more than 200 pounds (91 kg).

Asiatic black bears are sometimes called moon bears because the markings on their chest look like a **crescent** moon.

# FEEDING TIME!

All black bears are omnivores. This means they eat both plants and animals. Black bears all enjoy fruits, nuts, and honey. American black bears often eat grasses and acorns. Asiatic black bears tear the bark from trees to eat when food is hard to find.

Black bears sometimes eat animals that have already been killed by another predator. In other cases, they kill young animals, such as deer and moose. Black bears eat bugs, too. American black bears are also known for eating garbage left at campsites.

## —Bear Basics—

Black bears will eat whatever food they find. They even eat livestock, or farm animals. Sometimes, farmers try to kill black bears because they want to protect their livestock.

Black bears eat the most in summer and fall. In winter, they don't eat anything. They go into a kind of deep sleep, but they can wake up if they need to.

# BABY BLACK BEARS

Black bears are solitary animals, which means they most often live alone. One time this changes is during the mating season, which is when males and females come together to make babies. Most black bears mate in summer, but some Asiatic black bears have their mating season in early fall.

Baby black bears, which are called cubs, are born in winter, and they live with their mother after they're born. Asiatic black bear cubs stay with their mother longer than American black bear cubs.

Mother black bears teach their cubs how to find food and stay alive in the wild.

# AMERICAN BLACK BEARS AND PEOPLE

American black bears are common animals in North America. People often see them in the woods or near a campsite. However, it's important not to feed black bears. They can get used to human food and then start coming around people more often. This isn't safe for people or bears.

There are enough black bears in North America that hunting these animals for sport is allowed. American black bears don't often attack people. They'd much rather stay away from people if they can.

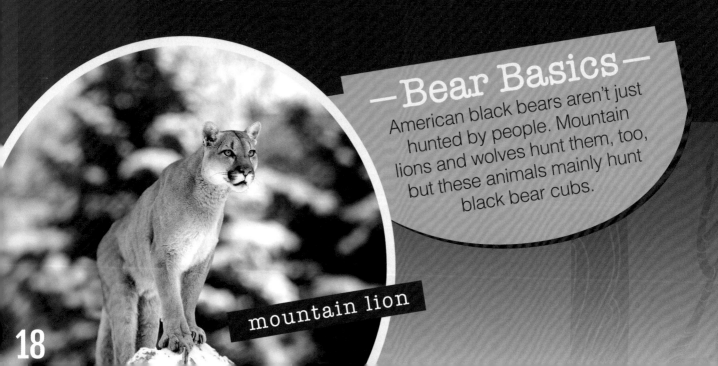

## —Bear Basics—

American black bears aren't just hunted by people. Mountain lions and wolves hunt them, too, but these animals mainly hunt black bear cubs.

mountain lion

The **population** of American black bears is still healthy, but it could **shrink** because of human activity. People not only hunt these animals, they cut down the forests where they live.

# BEARS IN DANGER

The population of American black bears may be healthy, but the population of Asiatic black bears is shrinking. These bears are often killed by Siberian tigers. People also hunt Asiatic black bears. Some of their body parts are used in Asian medicines. Hunters also kill Asiatic black bears for their paws and skin.

Asiatic black bears are in danger of losing the forests where they live because of building projects. Groups of Asiatic black bears are more **isolated** now than ever before. This makes it hard to study them in the wild.

## AMERICAN BLACK BEARS

- live throughout North America
- can be many different colors
- ears are closer together
- shorter fur
- cubs stay with mother for 16 months to two years
- hunted by mountain lions, wolves, and people
- population is healthy

## BOTH

- live mainly where there are trees
- use claws to climb trees
- omnivores
- go into a deep sleep during winter
- solitary animals
- cubs are born in winter
- generally have two or three cubs at a time

## ASIATIC BLACK BEARS

- live in small areas of Asia
- white or sandy-colored "V" on chest
- ears farther apart
- longer fur
- cubs stay with mother for up to three years
- hunted by Siberian tigers and people
- population is getting smaller and more isolated

American black bears and Asiatic black bears have many things in common, but they have important differences, too!

# BLACK BEARS AROUND THE WORLD

People are sometimes afraid of black bears, especially when they see them around a campsite or in a park. It's good to remember, though, that these bears hardly ever hurt people. In fact, people are much more of a danger to them than they are to us!

Whether they're found in the forests of North America or the mountains of Asia, black bears are important parts of wildlife communities around the world. People study them in zoos and watch them in the wild. Have you ever seen a black bear?

# GLOSSARY

**continental:** Being the mainland part of a country.

**crescent:** The shape of the part of the moon that can be seen when it is less than half full.

**depend:** To be determined by or based on.

**elevation:** Height above sea level.

**isolate:** To put or keep something in a place that is separate from others.

**population:** The number of animals that live in an area.

**protect:** Having to do with keeping someone or something safe from harm.

**range:** A set of things in a line, such as mountains.

**shrink:** To become smaller in amount or size.

**swampy:** Made up of land that is always wet and often partly covered with water.

# INDEX

# WEBSITES

Due to the changing nature of Internet links, PowerKids Press has developed an online list of websites related to the subject of this book. This site is updated regularly. Please use this link to access the list: www.powerkidslinks.com/bworld/black